Knowledge Apocalypse
Ancient Astronauts & The Search for Planet X

Apocalypse ("lifting of the veil" or "revelation") is a disclosure of something hidden from the majority of mankind in an era dominated by falsehood and misconception, i.e. the veil to be lifted.

Table of Contents

Intro by Jason Martell

Many people have a hard time conveying the impact this information has had on their life. This book will be an easy gateway for new people to get introduced to the ancient astronaut theory and the true nature of our human history. How can we ever expect to change as a race if we don't accept our place in the universe?

All the ancient cultures speak of a time when they had a connection with beings not from earth that were both spiritually and technologically more advanced then us. I often wonder why this disconnect with more advanced beings has taken place. Their impact on our lives is reflected in the information gathered in this book. A visit by an extraterrestrial race would show all humanity that we are not alone and never have been. This would have dramatic affects on world religion and how we perceive our place in the universe. Hopefully within our lifetime, we can make enough change and progress to be welcomed into the galactic inner circle as respected members.

Structures On Mars

One day in the 1996, I was attending college in San Diego, California, when someone tangentially mentioned to me that there were a "face" and "pyramids" on the surface of Mars. And that NASA had taken photographs of these objects.

I was of course very skeptical to this information and did not think much of it. If NASA had taken pictures of artificial structures on the surface of another planet, this would be the biggest discovery of our lifetime. This was the first time I had heard of Cydonia, the region of Mars where the face and pyramids are located. And since I have never seen this topic covered on MSNBC or CNN, I assumed it must be ludicrous.

When I looked at the photos of the Face and Pyramids on Mars, they seemed very familiar to something I had seen here on earth. The sphinx and pyramids in Egypt. I had just started to learn how to use the internet in 1996, so I began to curiously look into what NASA and other sub-contracted agencies of NASA were currently studying. It turns out the principal scientist in charge of the cameras we attach to the orbiters we send to mars are controlled by a company also located in San Diego, California, Malin Space Science Systems.

I contacted Dr. Malin to ask him about the Face and Pyramids on Mars and he was nice enough to respond to me directly. He stated "there is no evidence that the face and pyramids are artificial structures. We simply attribute them to sand and natural weather erosion." This answer really intrigued me because when I looked at the Cydonia region of Mars, the face, pyramids, and even other surrounding objects were clearly formed in some "artificial" way.

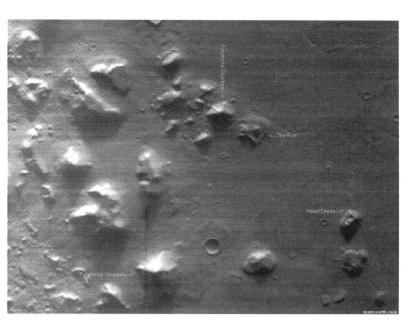

I began to look for answers outside of NASA to see if others were aware of these photographs and if any proper science had been done to explore if these could possibly be artificial structures. I was able to find 5-10 peer level review scientists that have PhD's in image analysis of satellite telemetry. People who did not work for NASA, but had the same level of education and experience. One of these people is Dr. Mark Carlotto, who used mathematical algorithms to detect Russian military troops and artillery from satellite telemetry over Russia. Running these algorithms on Russian satellite telemetry showed objects hidden by tarps or bushes still had a high probability of being artificial. Dr. Carlotto used these same mathematical algorithms on the satellite telemetry from the surface of Mars and found the Face and Pyramids to be over 98% probability of being artificial.

NASA never applied any level of scientific scrutiny to these structures and just quickly tried to say these objects were just a trick of light and shadow. However, we found that statement to be erroneous.

The first image NASA took of the Face On Mars was back in the 70's from their Viking Orbiter. When the image was beamed back to NASA headquarters, they quickly labeled the shot "Head" and said that they re-imaged the same location several hours later and the face was gone. WRONG ANSWER NASA!

It turns out that NASA had taken several images of the "head" from different orbital latitudes where the degree of the camera and the angle of the sun was different. And each time the face still is visible. It's a 3dimensional model carved in stone! Notice the shadow on the face in the below images is different in each image, but it still looks like a face.

 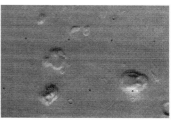

These images were located in the 80's by 2 researchers named Vincent Dipettrio, and Greg Molenar. They did further study to show that the large pyramidal structure near the face was expressing high level geometry to other structures in the area. This was also confirmed by several other independent researchers.

I become very fascinated with the face and wanted to know for myself weather this structure was man made. I downloaded every high-res image of the face I could get from NASA going back to the 70's Viking missions.

In looking at the face closely under magnification on a computer, I started to notice actual facial characteristics that I could recognize such as a nose, eyes, teeth, and even a head dress of some sort that could be a helmet or head ornament.

I started to ask myself "How could this be?, Why is it that not one of my friends or anyone I know is aware of this!"

It seemed the face was very badly eroded on the right side, but the left side still had very clear facial features. Knowing that all faces are A-symmetrical, I decided to run a few tests on the face.

When you look at your face in a mirror, only exposing half your face, you still see your face in the mirror. The reflected side of your face matches the part not shown in the mirror. This same practice used on the face on mars brings out some interesting details.

7

There are several images of the Face that NASA has taken in the past 30 years. I choose some of the more recent images shot in the 90's for this test. Interesting to note that the Face actually looks worse in more recent images. You would think that with improved camera technology, NASA would be able to produce clearer images of the face. For some reason the clearest images of the face are from the 70's. Is NASA trying to hide something?

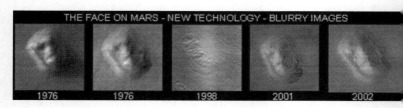

Back to the test....Taking the image you see here and mirroring the "left" and "right" side of the image produces some interesting results.

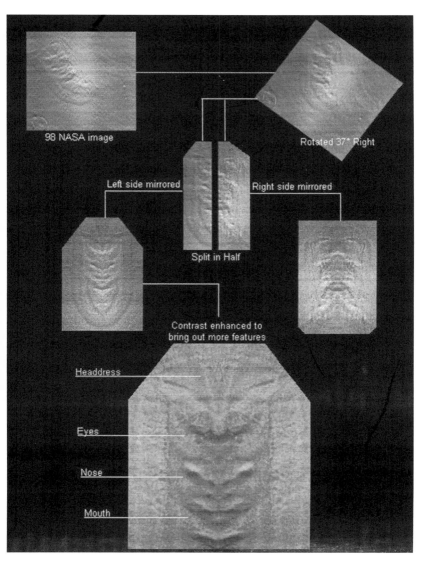

98 NASA image

Rotated 37° Right

Left side mirrored

Right side mirrored

Split in Half

Contrast enhanced to
bring out more features

Headdress

Eyes

Nose

Mouth

Looking at the right side which is using the more eroded
right part, you can still see clear facial characteristics
like eyes, nose, mouth, and overall semitry in its
appearance. Now look at the mirrored left half which is
not as eroded and shows much clearer features. Now we

9

begin to see the real detail. Even the outer lining of the head seems to have a strong resemblance to a head dress.

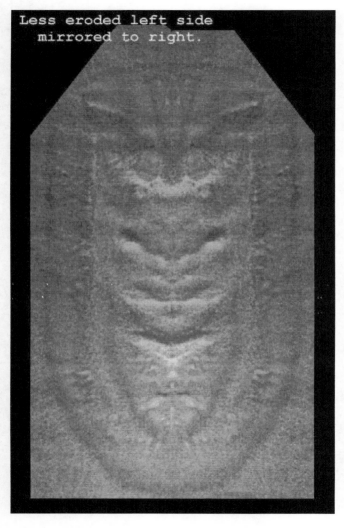

Less eroded left side mirrored to right.

The "Face" on Mars has now passed each test of artificiality yet proposed. These tests include a three dimensional structure, a lack of fractal patterns in the

10

image, non-random distribution of the nearby small mounds, proximity of other anomalous landforms, an apparent bilateral symmetry, being located on the martian equator, having a culturally significant orientation, and serving an apparent culturally significant purpose.

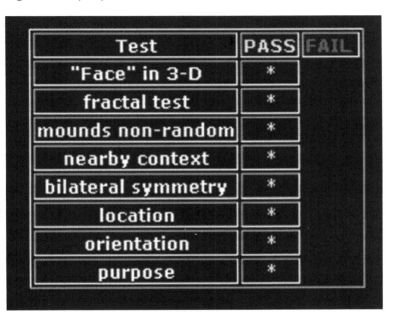

Test	PASS	FAIL
"Face" in 3-D	*	
fractal test	*	
mounds non-random	*	
nearby context	*	
bilateral symmetry	*	
location	*	
orientation	*	
purpose	*	

It would be an exaggeration to say that the case for artificiality is now compelling, and many thoughtful people will still find that conclusion less likely than all these "coincidences" put together. Yet the balance of the evidence, considered objectively, now weighs clearly in favor of artificiality over a natural origin of the Cydonian landforms.

Green on Mars?

NASA's pictures of the Gusev crater using the Mars Global Surveyor, and the more recent Odyssey mission using the Themis Camera reveal some interesting data.

The images taken show a dark mass that at first glance seems to have characteristics that resemble some sort of planet life.

Then in 2004, the European Space Agency took its first full color image of the Gusev crater. What made the ESA image so immediately interesting was the fact that the "dark mass" features seen streaking in portions of the floor of the 90-mile-wide Crater in the NASA imaging (left). They can now be seen in true color by ESA revealed by Mars Express (right) to be various amazing shades of green.

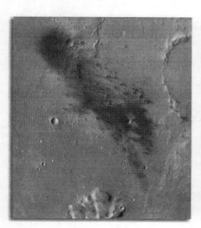 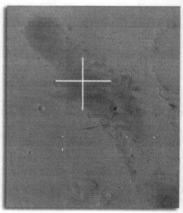

At Gusev, if the craters in the area were indeed harboring conditions conducive to some special algae growth – primarily, by extending below the local water table -- then one could easily speculate that as the algae mats within some craters grow in the Martian spring and summer, and ultimately reproduce, their spores are carried by the winds out of the craters ... to form the long, sinuous streaks across the intercrater surfaces observed from orbit! The "streaks," then, would simply be more colonies of algae from the craters ... spread by algae spores surviving for a time between the crater floors ....

However, deprived of crucial quantities of water and essential nutrients (which, in this scenario, would be concentrated on those crater floors), the migrating algae colonies between the craters quickly die ... and decompose. Through this process, they would inevitably release some of their bound organics – the hydrogen, carbon, etc. -- back into the atmosphere ... to be seen as significant quantities of methane gas.

During 2004 observations from the ESA Mars Express spacecraft in orbit around Mars, methane was detected in its atmosphere. And even more recently, Methane has been detected on Mars by three independent groups of scientists. And this could be a sign of life - indicating methane-producing bacteria.

Mars-Earth Connection

I started to reflect back on Egypt, with the sphinx and pyramids. There has to be a connection, a Mars-Earth Connection. (www.Mars-Earth.com).

It is certain, too, that the principal Giza monuments form an accurate terrestrial 'map' of the three stars of Orion's belt as these constellations appeared in 10,500 BC. Who could have been observing the skies over Giza in 10,500 BC and who, at that date, could have had the technical capacity to realize such monumental works as the Sphinx and the pyramids? Egyptologists assert there were no civilization on Earth at that time, let alone one capable of planning and building such immense, well engineered structures.

If they are right, why do the alignments of Giza so plainly and repetitively mirror the skies of the 11th millennium BC? There may be a 'terrestrial connection' between Giza and Cydonia - the region of Mars where the mysterious structures are located - perhaps a

common source that imparted the same legacy of
knowledge and symbolism on both worlds.

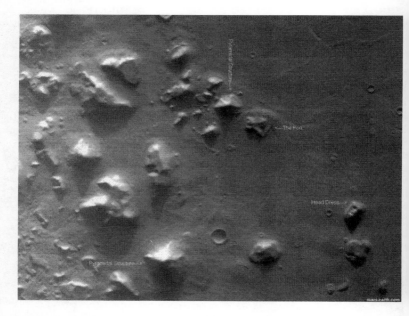

If the structures are intelligently created, then what is
their purpose? When you look closely at the image
above, you can clearly see what appears to be a terrain
difference right at about where a shore line would be if
the city was on the edge of land. The face is positioned
in a way that would be visible from the city. So are other
key features in this area, like the D&M pyramid.

Is this just coincidence? NOPE. The geology alone speaks for its self. Whether or not the surface difference is caused by water, I am not able to say since I am not a geologist. But, in my opinion just by looking at the image myself, and the anomalies in the region, it seems quite possible that Cydoina was built right at the edge of water. Just like we do on earth with waterfront property. Notice the color and knobby terrain near all the pyramidal structures which might indicate those were located on land. The face however is surrounded by less knobby, lighter color surface.

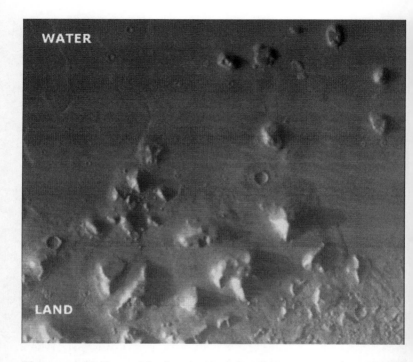

WATER

LAND

The more I thought about what it might mean that there is a Face and Pyramids on Mars, made me think about all the megalithic structures here on Earth. We have large stone monuments that are located on every continent yet we don't really know for sure who built them and for what purpose. A perfect example is the Giza Pyramids.

If you ask an Egyptologist "Who built the pyramids?" they will answer that ancient Egyptian slaves built the pyramids in a course of about 20 years. They base this on the wall carving and hieroglyphs which show the slaves moving large blocks of stone.

16

But the real question should be where are the tools they used? Large quarry sites from today use very large machinery to accomplish these large tasks. Where are the machines or advanced tools the slaves used? It is not enough to say 20,000 people working 20 years straight could have built the pyramids WITHOUT the use of large quarry sites or tools to excavate the stones used.

New evidence has risen that raises even more questions as to the actual purpose of the pyramids as well as their construction date. Using star mapping software on a PC, we can determine where the stars will be located at any specific time in the future or the past. This is useful for knowing that you can go outside your home at night at locate specific star constellations.

Using star mapping software over the Giza plateau shows us some interesting information about the 3 pyramids and sphinx. It turned out that in 10,500 BC the 3 pyramids of Giza are forming a terrestrial map of the Orion constellation. Also, on that exact date, the sphinx gazes east directly into the constellation of LEO, the lion.

Is this just coincidence? How could the Egyptian slaves from 2,500 BC build the Giza pyramids to precisely match the Orion Constellation from the year 10,500 BC?

There is also strong geological evidence that the sphinx has been heavily weathered by water sometime in its past. When was the last time it rained on the Giza dessert? Just over 10,000 years ago...

Megalithic Structures All Over The Earth

I have briefly covered here some of the characteristics around Giza that highlight evidence showing Giza is much older than we thought. So what about the other megalithic structures all over the earth?

I wanted to know, "Where is the oldest civilization on earth? Where do we really come from?" Everyone has heard of the idea that there was once a great continent known as Atlantis. And on this continent existed an advanced civilization. But over many 1000's of years, Atlantis was lost and some people claim that it sunk into the ocean. What if there was an advanced civilization at some point in the past around 10-15,000 years ago? It seems more likely that an "advanced civilization" would also be a global civilization, and we would see evidence of their technology all over the earth.

Some of the most recent data show hints that such a lost culture did exist from the discoveries of Kennewick Man, the red-haired mummies of Central Asia, the pale Ainu people of Japan, and the long faced stones of Easter Island, all feeding into the mythology of the South American red races who revered the long-eared, light-skinned, bearded, elder gods from the heavens.

The only other source for this information, would be the "Gods" gave this information to mankind. If you ask the most ancient civilization the Sumerians, about their knowledge they say " All we learned, we were taught by the Anunnaki." This word means "those who from heaven to earth came". We will discuss the term "Anunnaki" later in this book. You will see many references to them as likely candidates for the source of esoteric information.

If you look at Nazca, Stonehenge, Giza, Machu Picchu, Teotihuacan, and many other megalithic locations around the world we see evidence of monuments that are astronomically aligned with such precession it baffles modern scholars.

Baalbek

This MASSIVE ~3 million square foot stone platform contains huge stones, including "The Trilithitons' which each weigh ~1200 tons, that's 2.4 million pounds. Much later, the Greeks and Romans built their temples on top of it. Legend has it that the Sun god Helios landed upon the platform with his fire chariot. The site is also described in the ancient flood tale of Gilgamesh.

Stonehenge

Recent evidence dates the site to ~8000 B.C. The stones are perfectly constructed for predicting and sighting a wide variety of astronomical alignments including the precession of the equinoxes. There are a total of 60 standing stones and lintels , the classic Anunnaki sexagesimal number which is also embedded in our standard of time (60 seconds X 60 minutes=3600, the # of years in Nibiru's orbit).

Easter Island

22

Humongous carved stone heads weighing an average of 13.78 tons are arranged all over the island. There are no known written records to explain their purpose or origin. Some of the "moai" carved in the quarry are as much as 165 tons. Some suggest that the workers who "vandalized" the Anunnaki Nazca lines fled to Easter island and constructed the maoi with the techniques they learned from the Anunnaki.

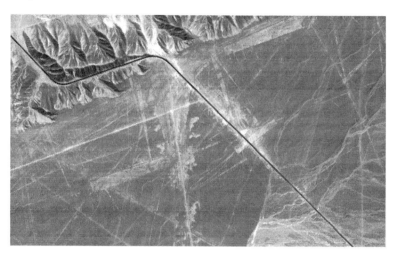

Nazca

The Nazca lines are spread over the arid plain and some stretch for several kilometers with almost no deviation in the straight line sections. The lines can only be seen from the air which, of course, suggests they were designed by a civilization with the power of flight.

Puma Punku

It seems to be the remains of a great wharf (for Lake Titicaca long ago lapped upon the shores of Tiahuanaco) and a massive, four-part, now collapsed building. One of the construction blocks from which the pier was fashioned weighs an estimated 440 tons (equal to nearly 600 full-size cars) and several other blocks lying about are between 100 and 150 tons. The quarry for these giant blocks was on the western shore of Titicaca, some ten miles away. There is no known technology in all the ancient world that could have transported stones of such massive weight and size.

Tiahuanaco

The massive structures at Tiahuanaco include over-engineered waterworks systems. The site apparently served as an Anunnaki metal-smelting center on the shores of Lake Titicaca, the highest navigable lake on Earth. The area is very reminiscent of Cydonia, another Anunnaki site on the former shores of an ancient body of water.

Teotihuacan

For centuries, Teotihuacán was the Mesoamerican region's cultural, religious, political, economic, and social center. The massive temples of the Sun, Moon, citadel, as well as, palaces, plazas, and paved streets were said built by a pre-Aymara civilization. Once again, another incredible site, the builders of which are unidentified before one considers the Anunnaki paradigm.

Maccu Picchu

Located 8,000 feet above sea level, Maccu Picchu was constructed out of massive stone blocks with great precision. Studies indicate it would be impossible for conventional means to lift the stones from quarries far down the mountains to such incredible heights. Also, the structures include a series of alignments which measure the precession of the equinoxes.

Okinawa

Over the last few years, divers and archaeologists have discovered an incredible series of massive stone ziggurats located approximately 80 feet under the sea. Clearly artificial and terraformed, these structures mimic other sites above ground on the islands of Japan. The last time these structures would have been above sea level and habitable was at least 10,000 years ago, before the end of the last ice age caused them to slip beneath the sea.

China

Up to one hundred massive earthen pyramids, solidified to rock hardness, are located within remote areas of China. Although the government does not allow many to come near them, photographs have surfaced revealing some of them to be as much as a mile on a side.

Cahokia

The ancient North American site includes large mounds of a variety of sizes and shapes. Recently drilling into one of them revealed a heretofore unknown and unexpected solid rock core which, it is believed, may be made of limestone. Efforts continue to reveal the hidden inner workings of these structures.

Earth's 1st Civilization – Sumer

My research led me back almost 6,000 years ago in our history to the oldest civilization we have on record. A fertile strip of land between the Tigris and Euphrates valley known as Sumer. Almost overnight, from right out of the stone age "Sumerian Civilization" emerged into the land that is now southern Iraq. It has been called Mesopotamia, Babylon, but the first culture were the Sumerians.

What is amazing about the Sumerian culture is we attribute over 100 of the 1st's needed for an advanced civilization. They were the first ones to create some of the following that we still use today.

Agriculture:

The Sumerians grew barley, chickpeas, lentils, millet, wheat, turnips, dates, onions, garlic, lettuce, leeks and mustard. They also raised cattle, sheep, goats, and pigs. They used oxen as their primary beasts of burden and donkeys as their primary transport animal. Sumerians hunted fish and fowl.

Sumerian agriculture depended heavily on irrigation. The irrigation was accomplished by the use of canals, channels, dykes, weirs, and reservoirs. The canals required frequent repair and continual removal of silt. The government required individuals to work on the canals, although the rich were able to exempt themselves.

Using the canals, farmers would flood their fields and then drain the water. Next they let oxen stomp the ground and kill weeds. They then dragged the fields with pickaxes. After drying, they plowed, harrowed, raked thrice, and pulverized with a mattock.

Sumerians harvested during the dry fall season in three-person teams consisting of a reaper, a binder, and a sheaf arranger. The farmers would use threshing wagons to separate the cereal heads from the stalks and then use threshing sleds to disengage the grain.

Math:

Sumerian mathematics refers to any mathematics of the people of Mesopotamia, from the days of the early Sumerians to the fall of Babylon in 539 BC. Sumerian mathematical texts are plentiful and well edited. In respect of time they fall in two distinct groups: one from the Old Sumerian period (1830-1531 BC), the other mainly Seleucid from the last three or four centuries B.C. In respect of content there is scarcely any difference between the two groups of texts. Thus Sumerian mathematics remained constant, in character and content, for nearly two millennia. In contrast to the scarcity of sources in Egyptian mathematics, our knowledge of Sumerian mathematics is derived from some 400 clay tablets unearthed since the 1850s. Written in Cuneiform script, tablets were inscribed while the clay was moist, and baked hard in an oven or by the heat of the sun. The majority of recovered clay tablets date from 1800 to 1600 BC, and cover topics which include fractions, algebra, quadratic and cubic equations and the Pythagorean theorem. The Sumerian tablet YBC 7289 gives an approximation to accurate to five decimal places.

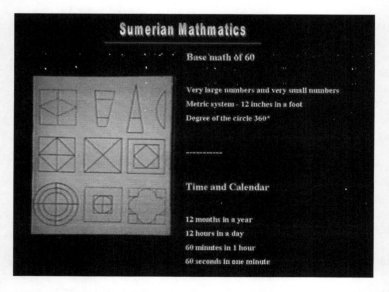

The Sumerian system of mathematics was sexagesimal (base-60) numeral system. From this we derive the modern day usage of 60 seconds in a minute, 60

minutes in an hour, and 360 (60×6) degrees in a circle. The Sumerians were able to make great advances in mathematics for two reasons. Firstly, the number 60 is a Highly composite number, having divisors 1, 2, 3, 4, 5, 6, 10, 12, 15, 20, 30 and 60, facilitating calculations with fractions. Additionally, unlike the Egyptians and Romans, the Sumerians and Indians had a true place-value system, where digits written in the left column represented larger values (much as in our base ten system: 734 = 7×100 + 3×10 + 4×1).

The Sumerians made extensive use of pre-calculated tables to assist with arithmetic. For example, two tablets found at Senkerah on the Euphrates in 1854, dating from 2000 BC, give lists of the squares of numbers up to 59 and the cubes of numbers up to 32. The Sumerians used the lists of squares together with the formulas to simplify multiplication.

The Sumerians did not have an algorithm for long division. Instead they based their method on the fact that together with a table of reciprocals. Numbers whose only prime factors are 2, 3 or 5 (known as 5-smooth or regular numbers) have finite reciprocals in sexagesimal notation, and tables with extensive lists of these reciprocals have been found.

As well as arithmetical calculations, Sumerian mathematicians also developed algebraic methods of solving equations. Once again, these were based on pre-calculated tables.

Schools:

Schools were attached to the main temple in the town and were referred to as the edubba. The head teacher maintained the title of school father or unmia. Each school father had assistants that were known as big brothers. It was the job of the school father to maintain focus, discipline, and provide most of the instruction. Big brothers would provide assistance to pupils, prepare clay tablets for writing, and at times also discipline the students. Students were continually reprimanded for mistakes. Humiliation and negative comments were commonplace. Students could also be hit with a stick.

Eventually, subjects other than scribing were added to the daily curriculum in schools. Students learned about mathematics, law, biology, astronomy, economics, agriculture and the Sumerian language. Creative writing only took place in schools. In Sumer, only upper class males went to school; girls were not allowed to attend. males would go to school for approximately twenty-five days a month and be in session year-round, from sunrise to sunset. Most males went to school to study to become scribes. Scribes recorded all business transactions, legal matters, and stories in ancient form of writing called cuneiform,. Being a scribe was a very prestigious and high-paying job in the Sumerian cities.

Students would spend their mornings copying myths and epics. Their afternoons focused on critiquing and refining their writing. The usage of numerous clay tablets and the constant copying of written material lead to the naming of Sumerian schools as "Tablet Houses."

Courts:

Although we don't know much about Sumerian law, scholars agree that the Code of Hammurabi, written by a Babylonian monarch, reproduces Sumerian law fairly exactly. Sumerian law, as represented in Hammurabi's code, was a law of exact revenge. This is revenge in kind: "an eye for an eye, a tooth for a tooth, a life for a life," and reveals to us that human law has as its fundamental basis revenge. Sumerian law was also only partly administered by the state; the victim had to bring the criminal to court. Once there, the court mediated the dispute, rendered a decision, and most of the time a court official would execute the sentence, but often it fell on the victim or the victim's family to enforce the sentence. Finally, Sumerian law recognized class distinctions; under Sumerian law, everyone was not equal under the law. Harming a priest or noble person was a far more serious crime than harming a slave or poor person; yet, the penalties assessed for a noble person who commits a crime were often far harsher than the penalties assessed for someone from the lower classes that committed the same crime.

Code of Hammurabi

Hammurabi's Law Code was the earliest known law code in existence. King Hammurabi is remembered for his 'Code' or collection of laws. It was modeled on existing laws, but this was the largest law code assembled. The Code has 282 provisions which dealt with many aspects of life, including family rights, trade, slavery, tariffs, taxes, prices and wages. The Code tells us much about Babylonian society. The Code of Hammurabi is inscribed on a stone slab over 2 meters (6ft) high. At the top, the King is shown receiving laws from the Babylonian sun god, Shamash.

The laws are not the same for rich and poor, but the weak were given some protection against the tyranny of the strong. The Code was not the only law code in Mesopotamia, but the only one written in stone. The code was based on retribution, not justice and varied unfairly between social classes.

THE CODE

1. If any one ensnare another, putting a ban upon him, but he can not prove it, then he that ensnared him shall be put to death.

2. If any one bring an accusation against a man, and the accused go to the river and leap into the river, if he sink in the river his accuser shall take possession of his house. But if the river prove that the accused is not guilty, and he escape unhurt, then he who had brought the accusation shall be put to death, while he who leaped into the river shall take possession of the house that had belonged to his accuser.

3. If any one bring an accusation of any crime before the elders, and does not prove what he has charged, he shall, if it be a capital offense charged, be put to death.

4. If he satisfy the elders to impose a fine of grain or money, he shall receive the fine that the action produces.

5. If a judge try a case, reach a decision, and present his judgment in writing; if later error shall appear in his decision, and it be through his own fault, then he shall pay twelve times the fine set by him in the case, and he shall be publicly removed from the judge's bench, and never again shall he sit there to render judgment.

Marriage:

In western society some aspects of modern family relationships and composition can be traced to ancient Mesopotamia and Babylonia. Ideas such as the wedding, marriage, and divorce began developing then. Through innumerable legal documents from the Sumerian to the Seleucid period, we see the individual as father, son, brother, or husband. The root of these relationships started with a proposal, followed by the marriage contract, and ending with the wedding. The young Mesopotamian couple then chose where to live. In certain circumstances, the male had to decide whether to have another wife or a concubine. In no time, the newlyweds begot children. The father, as the head of the family, had complete authority over them. This authority extended to such matters as adoption and inheritance. How big the family unit got depended on where in Mesopotamia it formed.

The family unit in Mesopotamia was small and restricted, although in certain regions of southern Babylonia clan like or even tribal organizations of some sort existed. In neo-Babylonian times, a measure of family consciousness appeared in the form of ancestral family names for identification purposes. The first step in creating a family unit, whether small or clan like, is of course the marriage. Ironically, for most of history, it left the prospective bride out of the decision-making process.

Marriage was regarded as a legal contract, and divorce as its breakup were similarly affected by official procedures. The future husband and his father-in-law agreed on a contract and if a divorce occurred, the father-in-law was entitled to satisfaction. The contract made between the suitor and the father of the expected bride stipulated a price for the maiden's hand. She received the sum given to the father. If the marriage did not produce children then the price the groom had paid for his wife was returned to him upon on her death, if it had not been returned previously. Lack of children was not the only reason for returning the price paid for the wife; her death could create a refund.

Once married, the girl became a full member of her future husband's family. If he died, she would marry one of his brothers or, if he lacked brothers, one of his near relatives. If these conditions did not take place, her father returned all his rights over her, and gave back all the presents that she had received except those consumed. Conversely, if the girl died, and her intended husband did not want to marry one of her sisters, he would take back all the presents that he had given her.

An agreement once reached indicated that the actual wedding ceremony could now take place.

I enjoy this proverb also found amongst Sumerian writing...."Men for his pleasure, Marriage. On thinking it over....Divorce".

Beer:

The oldest proven records of brewing are about 6,000 years old and refer to the Sumerians. It is said that the Sumerians discovered the fermentation process by chance. A seal around 4,000 years old is a Sumerian "Hymn to Ninkasi", the goddess of brewing. This "hymn" is also a recipe for making beer. No one knows today exactly how this occurred, but it could be that a piece of bread or grain became wet and a short time later, it began to ferment and a inebriating pulp resulted. These early accounts, with pictograms of what is recognizably barley, show bread being baked then crumbled into water to make a mash, which is then made into a drink that is recorded as having made people feel "exhilarated, wonderful and blissful!"   It could be that baked bread was a convenient method of storing and transporting a resource for making beer. The Sumerians were able to repeat this process and are the first civilized culture to brew beer. They had discovered a "divine drink" which certainly was a gift from the gods.

Astronomy:

They recorded the movements of the planets over 100's years. A Sumerian priest who could read the cuneiform text about astronomy could tell you 50 years in advance on what day there would be a lunar eclipse. They had very accurate astronomical information, which we have confirmed with our modern science. They actually listed the distance between the outer planets and correctly cited the color of the outer planets such as Uranus and

Neptune. When we sent the Galileo and Voyager probes into deep space in late 70's and early 80's they took the first color pictures on the outer planets. They exactly matched the Sumerian descriptions from 6,000 years ago as bluish-green planets.

Evidence to their knowledge can be seen is this amazing cylinder seal found in the British museum. Where as a backdrop to the drawing, we see our solar system with all the planets we know of and the sun listed correctly in the center. We did not know the sun was in the center of our solar system into the time of Copernicus and Galileo. They used advanced mathematics combined with new advances in the telescope to make these conclusions. But somehow the Sumerian culture from 6,000 years ago already knew this information. But how did they know?

They were the 1st ones to divide the heavens into 12 parts assigning each section of the sky with a symbol. Remember that number "12" as we will see has a key influence in our culture directly passed down from the Sumerian culture.

Writing:

The most important thing they created however was writing. Their form of writing was called cuneiform script. It consisted of someone using what looked like an over sized screw driver that they would then turn and twist into wet clay leaving the symbols. Cuneiform script has over 400 characters. That is pretty amazing for the 1st alphabet we have on record.

What is more amazing is what they wrote in the clay. They wrote most of their text in wet clay, then would place these clay tablets into a stove and make them into stone. They literally keyed the phrase "writing in stone".

Along with their stone tablet texts, were small round stone cylinder seals that had reversed carved images cut into the stone. And when pressed into wet clay they leave the positive imprinted image. It was quite an ingenious way to have an ancient printing press. They could easily create tablets and images to spread through out the culture.

They used this system of writing to record all kinds of information. Mainly it was used to record daily transactions of sales, or texts for education.

Medical Science:

Recent advances in DNA research have established that there was an Eve who lived about 250 to 270 thousand years ago, a first mother from who all modern humans stem, no matter what their racial heritage. [In 1987, scientists from the Universities of California and Michigan announced that all human beings descended from a single mitochondrial Eve: who lived in Africa.

Then came news a few years later that there also was an actual Adam. Finally, genetic advances made test-tube babies possible by mixing the male sperm with the female egg and re-implanting it.

The knowledge that we have acquired corroborates what the Sumerians knew 6,000 years ago. You wonder how is it possible, how could they know? How, as another example, could their symbol of the entwined serpents, that we still use today to denote medicine and healing and biology, be 6,000 years ago, the symbol of Enki, who engaged in genetic engineering to bring about the Adam? That was a symbol of the DNA, the double helix of DNA.

Notice in this image, on the top, the two entwined snakes and the ladder like ribbons between the serpents bodies.....does it remind you of anything?

Remember that these images are thousands of years old. Today we still use the image of the entwined serpent as a sign of medicine. This carried over from ancient times. What does the emblem of entwined serpents, the symbol for medicine and healing to this very day, represent?

The discovery by modern science of the double helix structure of DNA offers the answer: The entwined serpents emulated the structure of the genetic code, the secret knowledge of which enabled the creation of the Adam. The first man the Anunnaki created called the "Adam".

The Anunnaki - Those Who From Heaven to Earth Came

In the early 1900's British archeologists started doing excavations in the ancient Sumerian city of UR. Many of the artifacts and tablets spoke of beings called the Anunnaki and depicted these beings with wings. Why did ancient man depict the Anunnkai with wings? This seems very similar to angels in the modern bible. The answer is quite simple if we look at more modern references. In ancient times, man did not understand technology. So anything flying in the skies of earth had to be alive. Depicting the Anunnkai with wings leads me to believe the Sumerians were trying to say that the Anunnaki had the power of flight. Since ancient man did not

42

understand technology, they gave the Anunnaki wings to symbolically represent their power of flight.

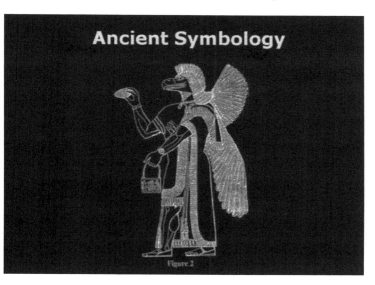

Ancient Symbology

Figure 2

If you look at modern references to when we landed the 1st Apollo mission on the moon, the words used to mark that event were" Houston, the Eagle has landed." Even the Apollo symbol was an eagle. Does this mean 6,000 years from now people will wonder why we were landing birds on the moon?

Modern Symbology

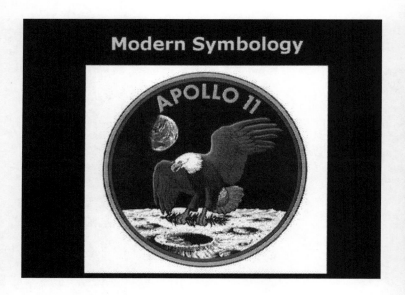

Most of the tablets describing the Anunnaki were thrown into a big MYTH pile and basically left untouched to this day.

However, the assistant curators of the museum found a set of tablets and began to decipher a very familiar story. On this ancient stone tablet was recorded a story about how a Sumerian man is chosen by god to build a great ship. To take his family and animals and even plants onto the boat because there was going to be a great flood. This tablet was 1000's of years older than any other biblical source of information. They had found the original source for "Noah's Ark".

The curator ran out of the room with his hands in the air shouting "I can't believe it, I can't believe it!"

The Epic of Gilgamesh is widely known today. The first modern translation of the epic was published in the early 1870s by George Smith who found the tablet. More recent translations into English include one undertaken with the assistance of the American novelist John Gardner, and John Maier, published in 1984. In 2001, Benjamin Foster produced a reading in the Norton Critical Edition Series that fills in many of the blanks of the standard edition with previous material.

Scholars found many tablets that seem to parallel stories found in our modern biblical texts. But since Sumer is the oldest recorded civilization, did we find the original source of biblical information? A very interesting twist to the Sumerian versions of the tales is they speak of a time when they lived amongst their living gods which they called the "Anunnaki".

They left many wall carving showing their interaction with these beings and depicted them with wings or coming down from heaven on a winged disk. At that time in the early 1900's when the British archeologists were finding these tablets and descriptions of the Anunnaki they considered all this information to be mythology.

Sumerian God coming to Earth

All the tablets that talked about the distance of the planets or what the outer planets looked like in space did not make any sense at the time. We did not discover Pluto until 1930. So many of these tablets talking about their GODS or events taking places in the 'Heavens" were thought of as myths, and put into a big pile and ignored for the most part by academia.

In the British museum alone, there are 1000's of Sumerian tablets and only about 1% of them have been translated up to this point. The tablets that haven been translated show that Sumerian knowledge was vast in many areas which modern science now confirms.

The area modern science has not yet been able to confirm is the stories they recorded about interaction with their living gods, the Anunnaki. The term Anunnaki, simply means those who from heaven to earth came. If you were to ask a Sumerian man, "How do you know all that you know?" they respond "All we know, we were taught by the Anunnaki." The depictions of the Anunnaki left by the Sumerians show us that we look very much like them. They even explained to the Sumerian priests "we made you in our image and after our likeness." (very similar to what we hear in the modern bible) These stories of creation are recorded in a series of 7 tablets that explain how our earth came to be, and why the Anunnkai had come to earth over 350,000 years ago. (See Atrahasis tablets)

The Anunnaki explained that they originally came to earth seeking gold and other precious elements. On their own rise to a technological civilization, the Anunnaki had damaged their planets atmosphere. They discovered that using fine particulates of gold, they could shoot this into the atmosphere to help patch the holes in the planets' ozone. We know gold has several key properties in how we use it today. We line all the astronauts spacesuit visors with gold as it is an excellent reflector of heat.

The Anunnaki found large veins of gold deposited in southern Africa. They dispatched a team of 50 Anunnaki to the surface of earth and began mining the gold out of the ground. They soon discovered the mining process was long and arduous. One of the leaders of the Anunnaki named Enlil suggested they create a worker race to mine the gold. He suggested using the primitive "ape man" that was evolving here on earth and to place their genetic marker on this creature. Enlil would use 20% of the primitive being and 80% of the Anunnaki genes to make a new being that would be "in their image and after their likeness" of the Anunnaki.

There were several images that accompanied the texts explaining this creation process. The texts explain how one of the chief scientists, Ninharsad tried several different attempts to create a working model. The 1st version the arm did not function, then in the 2nd model the kidneys were not working. Until finally she created a perfect model, they called Lu-Lu Amelu. There were pictograms that accompanied this text showing Ninharsad holding up the 1st working model, they called 'the adam'. The word Adam is seen in later times as a Hebrew word Adamu, which means worker. So the biblical tales we have today about Adam and Eve, now take on a different context that is much more detailed.

Once the Anunnaki had the working Lu Lu Amelu, they soon decided that they wanted to have a much larger work force and decided to then upgrade the Lu Lu Amelu to have male and female. By copying their own genetic code onto the primitive man, they created a new version of LuLu Amelu that was now male and female, just like the Anunnaki.

The Sumerian creation tales not only tell about the creation of man, but also the creation of earth. In the bible we have a consolidated version that says god created the heavens and earth in 7 days. Well the Sumerian "7 tablets of creation" tell a much more detailed story about the creation of earth.

The creation tablets state that our solar system was just starting to form and the planets had not become solid yet. An intruder planet appears and becomes gravitational influenced by the outer planets. Passing by Pluto, Uranus and Neptune. The intruder planet began to

48

travel towards the inner part of our solar system. Our primitive planet earth was labeled by the Sumerian as Tiamat. They explain that as the intruder planet passed through the inner part of the solar system, one of the large moons of this intruder planet collided into our primitive earth (Tiamat). The collision cracked Tiamat in half spewing out debris into the pattern we now see today as the asteroid belt. The bible calls this (the hammered out bracelet). After the collision, Tiamat is thrusted into a new orbit and the waters of Nibiru have intermingled with earth and life begins to arise already whole and complete. (panspermia)

The Sumerian creation tales explain some very key aspects to our modern understanding of cosmology, and possibly how life on earth began. For life to have naturally evolved here are earth would have taken billions of years longer than the recorded history of earth. The biological process of a living creature to take in nutrients and expel waste is extremely complex genetics. The idea that somehow life evolved on earth from primordial soup and a bolt of lighting is just not accepted anymore. That is equivalent to a tornado ripping through a junkyard and somehow magically assembling a 747, the odds are too great for that to be the answer.

Panspermia is the hypothesis that "seeds" of life exist already all over the Universe, that life on Earth may have originated through these "seeds", and that they may deliver or have delivered life to other habitable bodies.

The related but distinct idea of exogenesis is a more limited hypothesis that proposes life on Earth was transferred from elsewhere in the Universe but makes no prediction about how widespread it is. Because the term "exogenesis" is more well-known, it tends to be used in reference to what should strictly speaking be called panspermia.

The Sumerian creation tales explain how the waters of nibriu mingled with our earth. Could this be the answer to how life arrived on earth whole and complete? Nibiru being a much older planet, probably has had billions of years longer time for life to evolve. Or life to have arrived on Nibiru and then evolved much longer than life here on earth.

The creation tale goes on to explain that the planet Nibiru becomes a permanent member of our solar system on a highly elliptical orbit. The Sumerians recorded this orbit to be 3,600 years to complete and they called this a shar. A solar year for earth is 356 days to orbit the sun. Nibiru's orbit around the sun takes 3,600 years to complete one orbit.

If the Anunnaki come from Nibiru as the Sumerian have stated in their creation tales they would have a much longer life span compared to here on earth. As an example, someone from earth travels to Nibiru and stays on that planet for 1 year. When they return to earth, 3,600 years will have passed on earth. But the person returning to earth, has only aged 1 year. This point speaks to many of the biblical references with regards to ascending to heaven to enjoy a longer lifespan. Imagine if Jesus Christ was an Anunnaki and came here to earth and established his following. Then he leaves earth and returns to Nibiru for 1 year. When he returns back to earth, he has only aged 1 year, but it has been 3,600 years on earth.

If Nibiru does exist, our modern science might be able to see it. There are actual Sumerian tablets that show a man looking up while plowing a field. He is looking up to the sky with his hands shielding his eyes. In the sky you see circle emanating rays of light (the sun) and a cross emanating rays of light (nibiru). The Sumerian were aware of a time when they could actually see Nibiru as it came close to the inner part of our solar system.

50

The Search for Planet X

How might we see evidence for this planet being in our solar system? In the early 1990's, Dr. Robert Harrington the lead astronomer for the Naval Observatory in Washington suggested including another large planet in our solar system model. He could then explain many of the anomalies we currently see, such as why Uranus is tilted on its side. Or how Pluto and Neptune are possibly dislodged moons of Saturn. Dr. Harrington plotted an orbit of a planet with a very elliptical orbit coming out of the southern hemisphere towards the inner part of the solar system. His model very closely matched the description by the Sumerians of Nibiru being 4-8 times the size of earth and depicted as having a very elongated orbit. Dr. Harrington also noted that based upon orbital perturbations in the outer planets, there should be another large planet out there. This simply means that all the planets are being pulled in one direction by some force that would suggest there should be some large body as the cause.

In more recent times, the search for a planet x can now be placed under a larger astronomical interest in looking for extra-solar planets. (Planets that are not a part of our solar system). In this process we have also created many new classifications about stars and planets we are imaging deep in space.

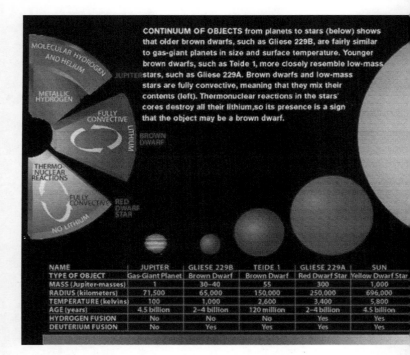

CONTINUUM OF OBJECTS from planets to stars (below) shows that older brown dwarfs, such as Gliese 229B, are fairly similar to gas-giant planets in size and surface temperature. Younger brown dwarfs, such as Teide 1, more closely resemble low-mass stars, such as Gliese 229A. Brown dwarfs and low-mass stars are fully convective, meaning that they mix their contents (left). Thermonuclear reactions in the stars' cores destroy all their lithium, so its presence is a sign that the object may be a brown dwarf.

NAME	JUPITER	GLIESE 229B	TEIDE 1	GLIESE 229A	SUN
TYPE OF OBJECT	Gas-Giant Planet	Brown Dwarf	Brown Dwarf	Red Dwarf Star	Yellow Dwarf Star
MASS (Jupiter-masses)	1	30-40	55	300	1,000
RADIUS (kilometers)	71,500	65,000	150,000	250,000	696,000
TEMPERATURE (kelvins)	100	1,000	2,600	3,400	5,800
AGE (years)	4.5 billion	2-4 billion	120 million	2-4 billion	4.5 billion
HYDROGEN FUSION	No	No	No	Yes	Yes
DEUTERIUM FUSION	No	Yes	Yes	Yes	Yes

Another fascinating and recent astronomical discovery is that almost all the external solar systems we have imaged with Hubble appear to be binary, having 2 suns. So it stands to reason our solar system is probably binary as well, having 2 suns. But our 2nd sun is a brown dwarf, a failed sun. This 2nd sun might also have planets and debris that orbit around it.

One theory proposed was by Dr. Richard Muller at Berkley University suggested a large planet called Nemesis may orbit our 2nd sun. There is a large asteroid belt also near our 2nd sun which this planet passes through. Dr. Muller suggested this Nemesis planet would periodically over millions of years dislodge comets and debris from the outer asteroid belt called the Ourt cloud. This debris would be hurled to the inner part of our solar system, and this is what Dr. Muller suggested caused the extinction of the dinosaurs.

Nemesis is a hypothetical hard-to see red dwarf star or brown dwarf, orbiting the Sun at a distance of about 50,000 to 100,000 AU (about 1-2 light years), somewhat beyond the Oort cloud. This star was originally postulated to exist as part of a hypothesis to explain a perceived cycle of mass extinctions in the geological record, which seem to occur once every 26 million years or so. In addition, observations by astronomers of the sharp edges of Oort clouds around other binary (double) star systems in contrast to the diffuse edges of the Oort clouds around single-star systems has prompted some scientists to also postulate that a dwarf star may be co-orbiting our sun. Counter-theories also exist that other forces (like the angular effect of the galactic gravity plane) may be the cause of the sharp-edged Oort cloud pattern around our own sun. To date the issue remains unsettled in the scientific community.

In 1984, paleontologists David Raup and Jack Sepkoski published a paper claiming that they had identified a statistical periodicity in extinction rates over the last 250 million years using various forms of time series analysis. They focused on the extinction intensity of fossil families of marine vertebrates, invertebrates, and protozoans, identifying 12 extinction events over the time period in question. The average time interval between extinction events was determined as 26 million years. At the time, two of the identified extinction events (Cretaceous-Tertiary and Late Eocene) could be shown to coincide with large impact events. Although Raup and Sepkoski could not identify the cause of their supposed periodicity, they suggested that there might be a non-terrestrial connection. The challenge to propose a mechanism was quickly addressed by several teams of astronomers.

Two teams of astronomers, Whitmire and Jackson, and Davis, Hut, and Muller, independently published similar hypotheses to explain Raup and Sepkoski's extinction periodicity in the same issue of the journal Nature. This hypothesis proposes that the sun may have an as yet undetected companion star in a highly elliptical orbit that periodically disturbs comets in the Oort cloud, causing a large increase in the number of comets visiting the inner solar system with a consequential increase in impact events on Earth. This became known as the Nemesis (or, more colorfully, Death Star) hypothesis.

If it does exist, the exact nature of Nemesis is uncertain. Richard A. Muller suggests that the most likely object is a red dwarf with magnitude between 7 and 12, while Daniel P. Whitmire and Albert A. Jackson argue for a brown dwarf. If a red dwarf, it would undoubtedly already exist in star catalogs, but its true nature would only be detectable by measuring its parallax; due to orbiting the Sun it would have a very low proper motion and would escape detection by proper motion surveys that have found stars like the 9th magnitude Barnard's star.

The last major extinction event was about 5 million years ago, so Muller posits that Nemesis is likely 1 to 1.5 light years away at present, and even has ideas of what area of the sky it might be in (supported by Yarris, 1987), near Hydra, based on a hypothetical orbit derived from original apogees of a number of atypical long-period comets that describe an orbital arc meeting the specifications of Muller's hypothesis.

Another recent theory called "Orpheus" suggests a large body entered our solar system in the past and collided with our earth. From that collision the debris formed into our current moon.

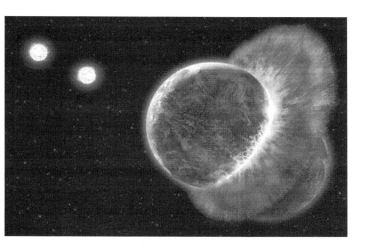

In 1898, George Howard Darwin made an early suggestion that the Earth and Moon had once been one body. Darwin's hypothesis was that a molten Moon had been spun from the Earth because of centrifugal forces, and this became the dominant academic explanation. Using Newtonian mechanics, he calculated that the Moon had actually orbited much closer in the past and was drifting away from the Earth. This drifting was later confirmed by American and Soviet experiments using laser ranging targets placed on the Moon.

However, Darwin's calculations could not resolve the mechanics required to trace the Moon backwards to the surface of the Earth. In 1946, Reginald Aldworth Daly of Harvard University challenged Darwin's explanation, adjusting it to postulate that the creation of the Moon was caused by an impact rather than centrifugal forces. Little attention was paid to Professor Daly's challenge until a conference on satellites in 1974 where it was reintroduced. It was then republished in Icarus in 1975 by Drs. William K. Hartmann and Donald R. Davis. Their models suggested that, at the end of the planet formation period, several satellite-sized bodies had formed that could collide with the planets or be captured. They proposed that one of these objects may have collided with the Earth, ejecting refractory, volatile-poor dust that could coalesce to form the Moon. This collision could help explain the unique geological properties of the Moon.

A similar approach was taken by Alfred G. W. Cameron and William Ward, who suggested that the Moon was formed by the tangential impact of a body the size of Mars. The outer silicates of the colliding body would mostly be vaporized, whereas a metallic core would not. Hence, most of the collisional material sent into orbit would consist of silicates, leaving the coalescing Moon deficient in iron. The more volatile materials that were emitted during the collision would likely escape the Solar System, whereas silicates would tend to coalesce.

In the last decade, we have seen a huge increase of interest from the astronomical community to the idea that a planet x does exist. There have been a flurry of press continuing reporting on new findings from independent teams claiming they may have found planet x.

Several smaller bodies have recently been found beyond Pluto. Most of them range from 800-1000km in radius. Nothing even close to the Sumerian descriptions of a planet 4-8 times the size of earth has yet to be located and imaged using our telescopes.

How do astronomers go about looking for a planet x? And who are these people?

The most recent finding at the time of writing this comes from a Japanese team lead by Dr. Tadashi Mukai. I contacted Dr. Mukai to ask about the size of Planet X he was projecting. He was kind enough to share this information below.

****

Dear Jason Martell-san,

Thank you for sending me information.

(Answer from Mukai) Its diameter is expected as 10,000-16,000km (roughly the same as the size of earth). Other details for Planet X is shown in the web site at http://www.org.kobe-u.ac.jp/cps/press080228_j.html Unfortunately, most of the news in Japanese, but you can get more from PDF file in item 1).

Best regards. Tadashi Mukai

****

One of the latest space telescopes deployed is called SIRTF - space infrared telescope facility, recently rename to Spitizer. This telescope is special in that it is kept below freezing temperatures and is able to tune its infrared capability in such a way as to match the temperature of these so called "dust clouds" deep in space allowing for a never seen before clarity deep into space.

John Carr of the Naval Research Laboratory, Washington, and Joan Najita of the National Optical Astronomy Observatory, Tucson, Arizona, developed a new technique using Spitzer's infrared spectrograph to measure and analyze the chemical composition of the gases within protoplanetary disks. These are flattened disks of gas and dust that encircle young stars. Scientists believe they provide the building materials for planets and moons and eventually, over millions of years, evolve into orbiting planetary systems like our own.

Ancient Planet X – Nibiru – Planet of the Crossing

In the early 1990's, calculations by the United States Naval Observatory have confirmed the orbital perturbation exhibited by Uranus and Neptune, which Dr. Thomas C Van Flandern, an astronomer at the observatory, says could be explained by "a single undiscovered planet". He and a colleague, Dr. Robert Harrington, calculate that the 10th planet should be two to five times more massive than Earth and have a highly elliptical orbit that takes it some 5 billion miles beyond that of Pluto.

We know today that beyond the giant planets Jupiter and Saturn lie more major planets, Uranus and Neptune, and a small planet, Pluto. But such knowledge is quite recent. Uranus was discovered, through the use of improved telescopes, in 1781. Neptune was pinpointed by astronomers (guided by mathematical calculations) in 1846. It became evident that Neptune was being subjected to an unknown gravitational pull, and in 1930 Pluto (was located). The latest advances in space imaging do not rely solely on orbital perturbations as the way for locating and identifying possible candidates for Planet X.

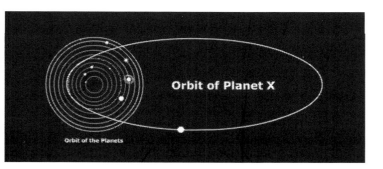

The 6,000 year old Sumerian descriptions of our solar system include one more planet they called "Nibiru", which means "Planet of the crossing". The descriptions of this planet by the Sumerians match precisely the specifications of "Planet X" (the Tenth Planet), which is currently being sought by astronomers in the depths of our own Solar System. Why has Planet X not been seen in recent times? Views from modern and ancient astronomy, which both suggest a highly elliptical, comet-like orbit, takes Planet X into the depths of space, well beyond the orbit of Pluto. We discovered Pluto with our telescopes just recently in 1930. Is it not possible that there are other forces at work on our solar system besides the nine planets we know of? Sumerian descriptions of Our Solar System are being confirmed with modern advances in science.

Pangea Explained By The Sumerians

To illustrate some of the amazing knowledge the Sumerians possessed 6,000 years ago, I will use a reference to something that to this day is still being taught by our education system. When the Earth was much older, we can determine the land mass was once a clumped together mass at one point in time. But due to the process known as "Continental Drift" or "Plate tectonics",the land clump was slowly pulled apart to where the current land masses are today.

PANGEA -- It Fits!

Explained 6,000 years ago by the Sumerians

We can see clear proof that the continents were all once connected by simply looking at a map of the Earth and seeing how the pieces fit. That would only mean that at one time, Earth was basically *half a planet*.

Where did the other half go? Why is Earth only half a planet? The diagrams shown here are descriptions from the Sumerians explaining how our Earth came to be... They state that the satellites of Planet X (Nibiru) as they called it, collided with our primitive Earth in the past. Creating the asteroid belt and forever becoming another member of our solar system in a comet like 3,600 year orbit around the sun.

In February, 1971, the United States launched Pioneer 10. Pioneer 10 scientists attached to it an engraved aluminum plaque. It attempts to tell whoever might find the plaque that Mankind is male and female, etc., and that (Pioneer 10) is from the 3rd planet of this Sun. Our astronomy is geared to the notion that Earth is the 3rd planet, which indeed it is if one begins the count from the center of our system, the Sun. But to someone nearing our solar system from the outside, the 1st planet to be encountered would be Pluto, the 2nd Neptune, the 3rd Uranus, the 4th Saturn, the 5th Jupiter, the 6th Mars .. and the Earth would be 7th.

The (12th) Planet's periodic appearance and disappearance from Earth's view confirms the assumption of its permanence in solar orbit.

The Mesopotamian texts spoke of the planet's periodic appearance as an anticipated, predictable, and observable event. The nearing planet, however, was expected to cause rains and flooding, as its strong gravitational effects have been known to do. Like the Mesopotamian savants, the Hebrew prophets considered the time of the planet's approaching Earth and becoming visible to Mankind as ushering in a new era.

Wherever the archaeologists uncovered the remains of Near Eastern peoples, the symbol of the Winged Disk was conspicuous, dominating temples and palaces, carved on rocks, etched on cylinder seals and painted on walls. It accompanied kings and priests, stood above their thrones, "hovered" above them in battle scenes, and was etched into their chariots.

Central to the religious beliefs and astronomy of the ancient world remained within the solar system and that its grand orbit returned it periodically to the Earth's vicinity. The pictograph sign for the 12th planet the "Planet of the Crossing", was a cross.

The ancient peoples not only expected the periodic arrival of the 12th planet, but also charted its advancing course. Many of the Sumerian Cylinder seals describe a planet whose orbit takes it far beyond Pluto, but also comes in from the SOUTH and moves in a clockwise direction - according to the Mesopotamian data.

The most intriguing part of this information is if we do confirm the existence of Planet X, we may very well have ancestors that live on this planet. All the religious texts that speak of beings coming down from the heavens would be put into a new light of understanding.

Many of the myths from ancient cultures might just turn out to be facts we confirm in the near future.

References

Zecharia Sitchin (1961)
The 12th Planet. HarperCollins

Graham Hancock (1995)
The Fingerprints of the Gods. 3 Rivers Press

Erik Von Daniken (1970)
Chariots of the Gods. Berkley Books

Igor Witkowski (2008)
Axis of the World, Adventures Unlimited Press

Lloyd Pye (1998)
Everything You Know is Wrong, Adamu Press

Graham Hancock (1996)
Fingerprints of the Gods, Three Rivers Press

David Hatcher Childress (May 2000)
Technology of the Gods, Adventures Unlimited Press

Made in the USA
Lexington, KY
15 December 2011